RESTORING TIBET

Global Action Plan
to Send the 14th
Dalai Lama Home

by

Evelyn Roberts Brooks

This book is intended to provide information and is not meant to prescribe, diagnose, treat, offer medical, psychological, or other professional advice. The author encourages you to explore this book if the material is of interest to you. You accept full responsibility for your own actions and choices. The author disclaims responsibility for what you might or might not do with the teachings or information in this book. Please use the information responsibly.

Restoring Tibet: Global Action Plan to Send the 14th Dalai Lama Home / Evelyn Roberts Brooks -- 1st ed.

SOCIAL MEDIA

Connect with Restoring Tibet (the Project):

restoringtibet.com
facebook.com/restoringtibet [Includes a blog in the "Notes" tab]
twitter.com/restoringtibet
pinterest.com/restoringtibet
YouTube meditations playlist: bit.ly/RTvideos

Contact Evelyn at:
facebook.com/restoringtibet
or
facebook.com/evelynbrooksauthor

CONTENTS

"Every day, think as you wake up, today I am fortunate to be alive,
I have a precious human life; I am not going to waste it.
I am going to use all my energies to develop myself,
to expand my heart out to others,
to achieve enlightenment for the benefit of all beings.
I am going to have kind thoughts towards others.
I am not going to get angry or think badly about others.
I am going to benefit others as much as I can."
– Dalai Lama

DEDICATION

For His Holiness the14th Dalai Lama,
and all Tibetan refugees,
with love

INTRODUCTION

September 11, 2016

Dear New and Old Friends of Tibet,

Fifteen years ago, terrorists attacked the World Trade Center.

The face of fear: Osama Bin Laden and like-minded, hate-based radicals.

The demonstration: Create destruction and a new Reign of Terror.

Instead of building walls and inadvertently creating more chaos when we want peace, I propose that we interrupt the cycle of fear.

I invite everyone in the personal development, spiritual growth communities, supporters of a free Tibet, and our millions of like-minded friends – _We the Peaceful_ – to band together and create a global manifestation of a different variety.

The face of peace: His Holiness the 14th Dalai Lama, Tenzin Gyatso.

The demonstration: Return the Dalai Lama home to Tibet.

Begin with the sense of wonderment at all our world has to offer us in the way of opportunities for growth and expansion. When we focus on fear, we immediately feel a sense of constriction rather than expansion, of doubt rather than faith, and that is why it is important to follow the spiritual processes that reside within this book for Restoring Tibet and bringing the Dalai Lama home again.

In each section you will be given practical methods of interacting with others so that together we raise the collective consciousness to such a degree that the manifestation of a free Tibet will indeed take place—instead of remaining on a "wish list" for countless millions of people around the world.

Since the inception of this idea for Restoring Tibet on January 29th of this year, I have been working twice daily with private meditations, with messages from spirit, with guidance on maintaining a feeling of joyful expectation despite the seeming lack of change in the outer world.

But there is something we can do to create change, by joining together in large numbers.

"Restoring Tibet" is a movement. It is an intention. It is a commitment.

Here's what it is not: a focus on all that has gone wrong.

In order to properly use the laws of the universe to create the change we desire, it is necessary to get our energy high up in the realm of joy. The easiest way to do this is to imagine we have already succeeded in our mission: the Dalai Lama is home in Tibet as its spiritual leader, along with thousands of former refugees.

In all aspects of this project, we will be forward-looking, and share only positive messages about the change we want to see.

Let us be <u>for</u> kindness.

Let us be <u>for</u> peace.

Let us be <u>for</u> freedom.

And let us open the doors for the Dalai Lama's return.

By speaking, feeling, and acting as if it is already true, we will stimulate the molecules of change and bring the concept of Restoring Tibet into actuality.

I am joyfully committed to manifesting this new reality of a free Tibet.

After nearly nine months of living and breathing this project, working alone on envisioning the Dalai Lama's peaceful return to Tibet, it is time for me to birth this baby and ask the global village of _We the Peaceful_ to join me in nurturing it and helping it to grow.

Please take a look at the Global Action Plan I propose. I hope you will feel inspired to join in meditation to manifest the Dalai Lama's journey home to Tibet. There is no cost to participate. To add your name to the movement, please go to Facebook.com/ RestoringTibet.

I invite you to be part of the biggest peaceful manifestation in history. All it takes is your willingness to say "_Yes!_"

Evelyn

Evelyn Roberts Brooks

P.S. I am not affiliated with the Office of the Dalai Lama or with any of the Tibetan support organizations around the world, although I sincerely welcome and hope for their endorsements and participation in Restoring Tibet.

STATEMENT OF INTENTION

Together we will create a new reality in which His Holiness the 14th Dalai Lama is easily and delightfully restored to Tibet.

We are connected to one another in the universal energy force, and we now use our creative power of manifestation to bring forth, from out of the field of infinite possibilities, the Dalai Lama's return to a free Tibet as its spiritual leader.

CHAPTER 1
ALL CREATION STARTS WITH AN IDEA

"There is a LIGHT in this world. A healing spirit more powerful than any darkness we may encounter. We sometime lose sight of this force when there is suffering, and too much pain. Then suddenly, the spirit will emerge through the lives of ordinary people who hear a call and answer in extraordinary ways."
—Richard Attenborough
(sometimes attributed to Mother Teresa)

An Idea Is Born

I woke up early on January 29, 2016 with an incredible idea, an audacious idea, an amazing idea...and I said "*YES*" to it.

The idea: *We should send the Dalai Lama home.*

My reaction: *Okay—what a great idea—let's do it!*

Because I have studied extensively the laws of the mind, when the idea came to me I knew at once that it meant I could be the one to fulfill the idea—but I had to say "*Yes.*"

Not, "*Yes, but I'm not even a Buddhist so I'm not qualified.*" Not, "*Yes, but my friends and family will think I've finally flipped.*" Simply: "*Yes.*" No qualifications, no conditions, no weighing the pros and cons and consulting the logical mind before replying. Just a simple decision.

I knew I didn't need to know the "*But how on earth will we do this?*"

steps at that point, because that all comes later, <u>after</u> the decision (not <u>before</u>, as most of us have been erroneously taught).

I didn't use a stopwatch, but I know that I said "*Yes*" on the next out-breath.

Although I'm an idea person and I have a constant inflow of creative ideas, this was the biggest idea by far, a B-HAG. That's for "Big Hairy Audacious Goal."

I realized that even though the idea presented itself to me seemingly "out of the blue," it had the full potential to come into manifestation with focused thought.

I understood later that the idea didn't randomly land at my feet: it was in answer to an affirmation I had been using daily regarding my life purpose. Actually it was a mission I'd accepted in childhood, affirming: "I help people be happier." But some months before getting this B-HAG, I'd changed my goal card wording to: "I help millions of people heal and be happier." Notice the difference? In response to my intention of helping <u>millions</u> of people heal, I was gifted with a beautiful idea for doing just that.

But I knew I couldn't do it alone: I'd need to attract others to join me.

Accepting the Project

When we accept an idea that comes to us, whether the idea is beneficial or destructive, we open the way for its realization in the physical realm. If we continue the manifestation process by thinking about the idea's outcome with great feeling (whether fear or love), that idea will blossom and become real.

I knew it was important to let the universe know that I was serious about my commitment and it wasn't a mere wish that I'd abandon if the whole thing started looking too difficult or cumbersome.

I moved into action to name it and to claim it. In the early weeks, my working title for the project was "The Dalai Lama Is Home Again." Then, as it came time to announce it on the Dalai Lama's birthday July 6th, I changed the name to "Restoring Tibet." That announcement was simply an announcement that the movement would launch on 9/11, and at that time I had no idea it would launch with this book. I thought maybe I was supposed to put together an online event with different speakers from the personal development community—but that project is on the wish list. Instead, here is the action plan. And it makes sense to me that the book comes first.

I understood I would be cloaking my work on the project in secrecy until I was guided to take the next steps. The secrecy was to protect my own energy from faltering if I were to discuss it prematurely with others who might not understand or support the project.

The first three weeks, I walked around mulling over the idea of restoring Tibet, loving it more and more as I began compiling pages and pages of notes and lists of ideas for events. I began gathering quotations that support the desired outcome, and I began creating content such as meditation audios and videos, and affirmations for my own daily use during the gestation period of this project.

Backstory on the Dalai Lama

I admit that at the time of getting the idea, my knowledge of the Dalai Lama, other than his message of compassion, love and kindness, was general in nature. In fact, to demonstrate my acceptance of the project, early in March 2016, I clicked over to his main Facebook page and "liked" it.

Notice the Dalai Lama has over 13 million "likes" on one page alone:

However, I believe my lack of emotional involvement in his current situation (other than feeling his exile is a condition it would be wonderful to reverse) made me an ideal candidate for receiving the idea. I had no major baggage in my mind to resist it or doubt it, or wish for it with such an intense residue of resentment and anger in my heart that I would actually repel it.

The Dalai Lama and thousands of native Tibetans fled their homeland in 1959, when the Red Army advanced in a path of destruction, torture and violence that has continued to today, in a clear attempt to wipe Tibet, its people and their heritage from the face of history.

The Dalai Lama states: "Almost six decades have passed since I left my homeland, Tibet, and became a refugee. Thanks to the kindness of the government and people of India, we Tibetans found a second home where we could live in dignity and freedom, able to keep our language, culture and Buddhist traditions alive."

If you wish more information about the history of and current status of the Tibetan issue, please start at the Dalai Lama's official website: dalailama.com

I hope that, after you have read this book and seen the possibilities of what we can create together, you will feel inspired to join in manifesting the journey home for the Dalai Lama and Tibetan refugees. There is no cost to participate. All it takes is a commitment to meditate daily, and I'll provide you with the meditation as well as other content you might find helpful for creating more joy in your own life at the same time.

Why Tibet?

You may be thinking that there are many important causes around the world that need our attention, and you'd be right. Perhaps you have a favorite cause that you support.

The Tibetan issue is unique in that, as with South African apartheid and Nelson Mandela, there is one person we think of in relationship to Tibet: the Dalai Lama. Thus it becomes a simple matter for us to focus our attention on a single goal of returning the Dalai Lama to his homeland, in peace.

Although there are some people in the world who would no doubt object to this plan of Restoring Tibet, first of all they would not be the type to read a spiritually-based book such as this, and secondly, I believe they are a small group of bullies who have gotten away with intimidating the rest of us for far too long.

Millions of people love the Dalai Lama and flock to see him in person. They wait for the privilege of a private interview. They eagerly read his books and listen to his teachings.

We can always count on the message from His Holiness to be one that is positive and loving.

Let's join together and create a peace manifesto. The Dalai Lama's return to Tibet is an ideal project in many ways.

In fact, the two-fold purpose of Restoring Tibet is to manifest the return to Tibet of the 14th Dalai Lama through the magnetic power of deep meditation, and also to create a highly visible sign of what it looks like to transition from war, divisiveness and struggle to a higher understanding of using the laws of the mind for the greater benefit of all people.

After we achieve Restoring Tibet, who knows what marvelous peaceful manifestations we can create together—there are no limits to the beautiful changes we can bring to life to benefit others. Poverty, hunger, homelessness, illiteracy, lack of education—all of these issues and more can be addressed and resolved with the power of our deliberately focused collective consciousness.

The Announcement

I announced the Restoring Tibet project on the Dalai Lama's birthday, July 6th, with this Birthday Card [Please see end of book for the card image] on Facebook, and a statement that the project would officially launch on 9/11/16, the 15th anniversary of the terrorist attacks in the U.S.A.

Once this project was public, I began posting videos, quotation images, and a blog at the Facebook page.

By the way, with that announcement on July 6, 2016, it was the first day I spoke of this project to anyone, privately or publicly. My Golden retriever, Sugar Bear, knew about it all along, of course, but she has never breathed a word of it.

A Springboard to Your Own Manifestations

During this process of Restoring Tibet, I invite you to open to ways of manifesting more of what you desire in your own life instead of accepting what seems to come into your experience out of sheer luck (good or bad).

Doing so will broaden your participation in the project, and also give you the necessary feedback and encouragement to keep going. When you enjoy the positive manifestation process, you'll begin to believe in it and practice it as a way of life.

Without struggle, you'll simply release the old habits of worry, doubt, and discouragement, and then you'll see the changes you've been longing for in your own greater success and happiness.

Instead of dreaming of something that we wistfully believe will never happen, with the laws of the mind, we know how to step into action. We begin the deliberate manifestation process, which may be readily understood intellectually but not so readily followed.

It is not that we are incapable of manifesting all we want; it is simply that we have inadvertently trained our thinking habits to go in the wrong direction, thus bringing us results that aren't always to our liking.

Focus on what you desire, make it feel real to yourself, expect it to come to you, and in that faith that what you want is indeed yours for the taking, take inspired action. These techniques and processes will be fully explained and outlined in the pages to come.

CHAPTER 2
THE DALAI LAMA, IN A BOX
LABELED "EXILED"

I know why the caged bird sings, ah me,
When his wing is bruised and his bosom sore,
When he beats his bars and he would be free;
It is not a carol of joy or glee,
But a prayer that he sends from his heart's deep core,
But a plea, that upward to Heaven he flings—
I know why the caged bird sings!
—Paul Laurence Dunbar, from his poem "Sympathy"

When you think of the Dalai Lama, what image comes to mind?

- A smiling man in a Tibetan Buddhist monk's red robe who shares an intensely peaceful and uplifting message of love, compassion and kindness.
- A brave elderly man in exile, who hasn't seen his homeland since he was a young man, at that time both spiritual and temporal leader of Tibet.
- Recipient of the 1989 Nobel Peace Prize.

Since most of us never learned the power of our words, we often describe the Dalai Lama as being a man in exile who can never return to his homeland.

We put him in a box. Not on purpose, but with the power of our words and the energy of the mind pictures we share globally.

Our collective consciousness has kept the Dalai Lama in a box labeled: "It's such a shame. He's a Nobel Peace Prize winner, but he can't even go home. He had to flee Tibet for his life, to escape the Chinese Communists who overran his country. He is in exile. He'll never see Tibet again!"

Together, we can and will release him from the old box with a NEW collective consciousness of freedom, joy and expansion as we grow into a worldview of peace.

This does not mean we ignore the reality of Tibetan suffering and destruction of their way of life that goes on today, but if we continue to label Tibetans as victims of torture, atrocities, injustice and more, then they cannot escape that box and we inadvertently perpetuate the very treatment we decry. That is how powerful our thought energy is!

We tend to take our freedoms for granted, until they are snatched away. We tend to think "someone else" will step up and lead the march forward towards justice. We tend to think it's not our job, that an issue is too big and must be handled by governments. We tend to feel helpless, fearing there is nothing much we can do other than donate to the wonderful organizations that support Tibetans in crisis.

We the Peaceful have the power to manifest change.

Let's collapse that box of injustice with waves of manifestation.

Imagine a peace-loving man is floating on a raft on a placid lake, without an oar or a paddle or a sail. He would like to reach the other shore, but it seems impossible.

There's a tall concrete barrier across the middle of the lake. It goes all the way to the bottom, so he can't dive under it. It's tall and slippery with no hand- or toe-holds, so he can't climb over it.

But then, first one and then another swimmer dives into the water behind the raft and heads toward it. They create waves. More and more swimmers leap in, adding to the power and height of the waves, until that raft is simply lifted up and over the barrier and the man on his raft glides into the far-off shore.

By swimming together and creating higher and higher swells, the group succeeded where one person's efforts could not. And yet, each swimmer also increased his or her own strength and experienced the satisfaction of being part of the collective effort.

Manifesting the Dalai Lama's return to Tibet will benefit all participants because, as they learn how to manifest the wish fulfilled as a group, they will learn how to harness the power of thought in all areas of their own lives.

In Chapter 1 I tried to give just enough of an overview of the Tibetan issue to explain the need for this project, Restoring Tibet, for those who might not be familiar with the Dalai Lama's reality. However, the events and other material for this project will never include a "serious" moment where we sadly turn our attention (and our manifesting energy) towards the past.

Joy, joy, joy must be the ever-present theme.

In the same way I can look back from today and tell you about something that happened in my past, by projecting my thoughts into the future, I can look back from the vantage point of completion and see this project unfold successfully.

Here is the defining moment that in my mind indicates the wish fulfilled: I am landing at the Lhasa airport with the Dalai Lama and members of his team who flew with us from India. My smile is joyous as I say to the Dalai Lama, "Welcome home, Your Holiness. Welcome home—to Tibet!"

We did it! It is done! Thank you...thank you...thank you!

I feel and experience the bright energy and joy of this airport scene as completely real–because it IS real in the metaphysical or thought realm.

Our simple task is to 1) join together to create a vivid picture of the Dalai Lama back home in Tibet, and 2) celebrate the restoration of Tibet in advance as if it's already true today.

Thus, with the subconscious power of manifestation, we will collectively out-picture our desire and make the Dalai Lama's return to Tibet real and true in the physical dimension.

Some months after I'd begun work on this project and wondering how I would manage to attract all the people necessary to be on the team with me, I noticed the daily quote from Abraham-Hicks in my inbox had pertinent advice for Restoring Tibet: "It's not your work to make anything happen. It's your work to dream it and let it happen. Law of Attraction will make it happen. In your joy, you create something, and then you maintain your vibrational harmony with it, and the Universe must find a way to bring it about. That's the promise of Law of Attraction."

History has shown what happens when people predict and believe in war and violence, and then when that same prediction begins a slow turn towards the hope of resolution. The reason World War Two is not still raging these many years later, although there are outcroppings of war going on all around the world in many different pockets, is that more and more people COLLECTIVELY began believing, "The war is ending!"

They turned their attention toward peace time projects and talked about how good the recovery would feel even though it would be a challenge. They began to envision how they would act in their daily lives in peace instead of in war.

Our project of returning the Dalai Lama to Tibet will access this same powerful process of turning the tide of thought and thus changing the outcome. This project has the potential to help millions of people understand the collective power of the human mind to affect good or evil depending on the direction we turn our focus.

Fear within our hearts expresses outward in our environment—not just in our own immediate circle of life, but globally as a dominant thinking habit shared by millions.

Now, imagine the power of turning our thoughts toward love, peace, humanitarian ideals, and freedom.

The time is right to orchestrate the Dalai Lama's return home with the unlimited power of the collective human mind as his vehicle. The process will be swift. It will not take years of struggle. It will be a joyful manifestation, pure and simple.

My goal: to breathe life into this project and easily attract participants. Together we WILL bring the Dalai Lama home, easily and delightfully.

CHAPTER 3
THE MAGNETIC PULL TOWARD HOME

"If we have no peace, it is because
we have forgotten that we belong to each other."
—Mother Teresa (now Saint Teresa)

Throughout the world, the concept of "home sweet home" is readily understood in a positive way in all cultures.

Where did "Dorothy" (in *The Wizard of Oz* yearn to go? Home.

Where does a child run to? Home.

Where do we flock to for holidays, celebrations, milestones, and understanding? Home.

Where are we eager to return to after a business trip or a vacation that has come to a fatigued end? Home.

What do people long for when they are taken away from it unwillingly due to disease, war, imprisonment, exile, or because of a far-off job? Home.

Nomads stay inside their own homeland, traversing within its boundaries.

Who do we feel sorry for? People with no home.

Even when people leave home to strike out on their own, and even if they turn their backs on their home of origin, they create a new home life with new friends.

Home, home, home. We feel the magnetic pull in our hearts. It resonates with our emotional DNA.

The focus of this project will be on returning the Dalai Lama home.

We will tap into the universal desire for home that everyone is familiar with.

This longing is expressed in countless songs, films, and everyday language: *I want to go home. Take me home. I'll be home soon. See you at home. Hurry home–I'll be waiting!*

It is natural to wish for home and the comfort that it represents to all humans.

The call to send the Dalai Lama home is one that will be recognized and gravitated towards immediately by many people who will feel curiously drawn to the project, and then want to participate.

During this project, participants will learn how to better use the law of attraction to create more joy, prosperity, and happiness in their own lives, too. It is the same process of manifestation that we'll use for Restoring Tibet, just on a different scale, and the steps will be readily adaptable to each individual's personal goals.

CHAPTER 4
THE PLAN TO SEND THE DALAI LAMA HOME

"Everything you want is out there waiting for you to ask.
Everything you want also wants you.
But you have to take action to get it."
—Jack Canfield

THE PLAN

By combining our magnetic power of manifestation, we will bring forth, from out of the field of infinite possibilities, the Dalai Lama's return to Tibet.

We will collectively create the biggest <u>positive</u> demonstration in history. (Up until now the biggest demonstrations have been World War One and World War Two.)

We will join globally in the vibrational energy of focused "collective consciousness" meditations and online events (including grassroots get-togethers around the world) to celebrate in advance the Dalai Lama's return to Tibet.

We will bring the Dalai Lama home by 1) visualizing he is already living in Tibet as Tibet's Spiritual Leader, and then 2) allowing the law of attraction to open the doors for his return.

CHAPTER 5
THE CASE <u>FOR</u> IT

"Take the first step in faith.
You don't have to see the whole staircase.
Just take the first step."
—Martin Luther King Jr.

THE PLAN, REITERATED:

By combining our magnetic power of manifestation, we will bring forth, from out of the field of infinite possibilities, the Dalai Lama's return to Tibet.

We will collectively create the biggest <u>positive</u> demonstration in history. (Up until now the biggest demonstrations have been World War One and World War Two.)

We will join globally in the vibrational energy of focused "collective consciousness" meditations and online events (including grassroots get-togethers around the world) to celebrate in advance the Dalai Lama's return to Tibet.

We will bring the Dalai Lama home by 1) visualizing he is already living in Tibet as Tibet's Spiritual Leader, and then 2) allowing the law of attraction to open the doors for his return.

THE CASE IN FAVOR OF RESTORING TIBET:

The Dalai Lama's "Middle-Way" Approach

From the Dalai Lama's website:

Question: Do you think you will ever be able to return to Tibet?

Answer: Yes, I remain optimistic that I will be able to return to Tibet. China is in the process of changing. If you compare China today to ten or twenty years ago, there is tremendous change. China is no longer isolated. It is part of the world community. Global interdependence, especially in terms of economics and environment make it impossible for nations to remain isolated. Besides, I am not seeking separation from China. I am committed to my middle-way approach whereby Tibet remains within the People's Republic of China enjoying a high degree of self-rule or autonomy. I firmly believe that this is of mutual benefit both to the Tibetans as well as to the Chinese. We Tibetans will be able to develop Tibet with China's assistance, while at the same time preserving our own unique culture, including spirituality, and our delicate environment. By amicably resolving the Tibetan issue, China will be able to contribute to her own unity and stability.

Neale Donald Walsch on Changing Non-Beneficial Worldwide Conditions

"Nothing that has been inflicted upon humanity by humanity is impossible for humanity to reverse."

"The larger the creation, the more power will be required to modify it. If we are talking about you being hungry, you can modify that creation relatively easily. If we are talking about world hunger, it will take more power (that is, more of you) to alter the creation, to recreate it anew. This is something most humans have been to date unwilling to do. These and other non-beneficial worldwide conditions, all created by humanity, exist not because they cannot be changed, but because there has not been the collective will to do so. Where there is a will, there is a way."

"Everything is energy. When you want for the whole world what you want for yourself—peace, joy, wisdom, happiness, and love—you multiply the energy you send out. When you do this at the same time that many others are doing it, you multiply your multiplication. You have increased your Impact Potential exponentially. You have literally harnessed the power of God. ('Wherever two or more are gathered, there am I.') This is important, because with regard to the challenges facing the world, the axiom is: The energy that creates the solution must be equal to the energy that creates the problem."

Bob Proctor on How to Do the Seemingly Impossible

"If you can see it then you can do it. How are you going to do it? Well, you'll be able to tell the person that after you do it. It's not all locked up in your intellect. It's locked up in faith. It's locked up in the belief that if you hold the idea in your mind, you'll move into the vibration that will attract it.

"That's why you've got to understand the laws. You've got to understand your relationship to the laws. And you've got to know that you can do it. Where will the money come from? Wherever it is right now! You will attract it."

Napoleon Hill on Man's Power to Achieve the Desired Outcome

"Whatever the mind can conceive and believe, it can achieve."

Joe Vitale on Creating World Peace

"I began to feel that my sole job in life is to say 'I love you' to anything that came my way, whether I saw it as good or bad. The more I could dissolve the limiting programs I saw or felt, the more I could achieve the state of zero limits and bring peace to the planet through me."

Florence Scovel Shinn on Man's Dominion over Mind, Body and Affairs

"The soul is the subconscious mind, and it must be 'saved' from wrong thinking. In the twenty-third psalm, we read: 'He restoreth my soul.' This means that the subconscious mind or soul, must be restored with the right ideas, and the 'mystical marriage' is the marriage of the soul and the spirit, or the subconscious and superconscious mind.

"They must be one. When the subconscious is flooded with the perfect ideas of the superconscious, God and man are one. 'I and the Father are one.' That is, he is one with the realm of perfect ideas; he is the man made in God's likeness and image (imagination) and is given power and dominion over all created things, his mind, body and affairs."

Wayne Dyer on Aligning Your Beliefs with Miracles

"Every thought you have impacts you. Shift from a thought that weakens to one that strengthens you."

"When you stay on purpose and refuse to be discouraged by fear, you align with the Infinite Self, in which all possibilities exist."

"When you are able to shift your inner awareness to how you can serve others, and when you make this the central focus of your life, you will then be in a position to know true miracles in your progress toward prosperity."

"Once you start to make the transformational awakening journey, there is no going back. You develop a knowledge that is so powerful that you will wonder how you could have lived any other way."

"When you know and feel the miracle that you are, you become certain that nothing is impossible for you."

Mary Morrissey on Creating with Your Future Memory of the Event

"Tap into the wavelength of the already done-ness."

Joseph Murphy on the Need for a Clear-Cut Idea

"Your failure to get results may also arise from such statements as: 'Things are getting worse.' 'I will never get an answer.' 'I see no way out.' 'It is hopeless.' 'I don't know what to do.' 'I'm all mixed up.' When you use such statements, you get no response or cooperation from your subconscious mind."

"If you get into a taxi and give half a dozen different directions to the driver in five minutes, he would become hopelessly confused and probably would refuse to take you anywhere. It is the same when working with your subconscious mind. There must be a clear-cut idea in your mind."

Pam Grout on Good Timing

"It's time to use our thoughts and consciousness to leverage magic."

"The fact that your thoughts are energy waves being broadcast out into this giant field of infinite potentiality is something you should be aware of and deploying on a moment-by-moment basis."

"By relying on cataloged lessons from your family, your culture, and your past, you miss the teeming energy available in the atomic now. There is great substance within each present moment, just waiting to explode with goodness and magic and blessings. But by reapplying old, often inappropriate 'cultural paradigms,' you miss the magic—you completely overlook all the life-empowering data that's trying to stream to you from your inner, nonphysical self. This traps you in a web of defensive, limiting perceptions."

"At every moment, we make the choice where we focus our energy. Always. One hundred percent of the time."

Vishen Lakhiani on Changing the World

"Extraordinary minds are not content to merely be in the world. They have a calling, a pull, to shift things. At this point in your journey toward the extraordinary, you may begin feeling an urge to shake up the culturescape by creating new models, new ideas, and new ways of life and living that move others to new places, too. You go from escaping the culturescape to returning to it and helping it evolve. All extraordinary minds go through this passage. They return to shake things up and change things. But this is no small feat."

Neville Goddard on Prayerful Yielding to the Wish Fulfilled

"Your prayer must be answered if you assume the feeling that would be yours were you already in possession of your objective. The moment you accept the wish as an accomplished fact the subconscious finds means for its realization. To pray successfully then, you must yield to the wish, that is, feel the wish fulfilled."

Thomas Troward on the Realization Process

"Having seen and felt the end, you have willed the means to the realization of the end."

Genevieve Behrend on the Power of Man's Mental Pictures

"All you have to do is to make such a mental picture of your heart's desire, and hold it cheerfully in place with your will, always conscious that the same Infinite Power which brought the universe into existence brought you into form for the purpose of enjoying Itself in and through you.

"And since it is all Life, Love, Light, Power, Peace, Beauty, and Joy, and is the only Creative Power there is, the form it takes in and through you depends upon the direction given it by your thought."

Amit Goswami on Quantum Creativity and Alignment

"Within one undivided consciousness, there are four worlds of quantum possibilities: the material world that we navigate with our senses, the vital world whose energies we feel, the mental world in which we think and process meaning, and the world of supramental archetypes that we intuit—truth, beauty, love, etc."

"If reality is my possibility, the possibility of consciousness itself, then immediately comes the question of how can I change it? How can I make it better? How can I make it happier? In the old thinking, I cannot change anything, because I don't have any role at all, in reality. Reality is already there. It's material objects moving in their own way, from deterministic lives. I, the experiencer, have no role at all. In the new view, yes, mathematics can give us something; it gives us the possibilities that all this movement can assume. But it cannot give us the actual experience that I'll be having in my consciousness. I choose that experience, and therefore, literally, I create my own reality."

Richard Dotts on Magical Manifestations

"The Universe always knows the best, most direct and most harmonious ways (the path of least resistance) to deliver your innermost desires to you. So leave this part of the equation to the Universe. Figuring out how it will come to you, or through which channel it will come to you, is unnecessary and only delays the manifestation process."

CHAPTER 6
THE CASE <u>AGAINST</u> IT

"You never really understand a person
until you consider things from his point of view ...
until you climb into his skin and walk around in it."
—*Atticus Finch* (from *To Kill a Mockingbird* by Harper Lee)

THE PLAN, REITERATED:

By combining our magnetic power of manifestation, we will bring forth, from out of the field of infinite possibilities, the Dalai Lama's return to Tibet.

We will collectively create the biggest <u>positive</u> demonstration in history. (Up until now the biggest demonstrations have been World War One and World War Two.)

We will join globally in the vibrational energy of focused "collective consciousness" meditations and online events (including grassroots get-togethers around the world) to celebrate in advance the Dalai Lama's return to Tibet.

We will bring the Dalai Lama home by 1) visualizing he is already living in Tibet as Tibet's Spiritual Leader, and then 2) allowing the law of attraction to open the doors for his return.

THE CASE IN OPPOSITION TO RESTORING TIBET:

An Apt Quotation from the Dalai Lama

"Silence is sometimes the best answer."

CHAPTER 7
THE QUANTUM POWER OF
INTERCONNECTIVITY

"All your experiences, all your actions,
and all the events and circumstances of your life
are but the reflections and reactions to your own thought."
—Joseph Murphy

From The Holographic Universe: The Revolutionary Theory of Reality *by Michael Talbot*

"...it may be that our thoughts are constantly affecting the subtle energetic levels of the holographic universe, but only emotionally powerful thoughts, such as the ones that accompany moments of crisis and transformation—the kind of events that seem to engender synchronicities—are potent enough to manifest as a series of coincidences in physical reality."

***

"One thing that we do know is that in a holographic universe, a universe in which separateness ceases to exist and the innermost processes of the psyche can spill over and become as much a part of the objective landscape as the flowers and the trees, reality itself becomes little more than a mass shared dream. In the higher dimensions of existence, these dreamlike aspects become even more apparent, and indeed numerous traditions have commented on this fact. The Tibetan Book of the Dead repeatedly stresses the dreamlike nature of the afterlife realm, and this is also, of course, why the Australian aborigines refer to it as the dreamtime. Once we accept this notion, that reality at all levels is omnijective and has the same ontological status as a dream, the question becomes, *Whose dream is it?*"

***

"But are we being dreamed by a single divine intelligence, by God, or are we being dreamed by the collective consciousness of all things—by all the electrons, Z particles, butterflies, neutron stars, sea cucumbers, human and nonhuman intelligences in the universe? Here again we collide headlong into the bars of our own conceptual limitations, for in a holographic universe this question is meaningless. We cannot ask if the part is creating the whole, or the whole is creating the part because *the part is the whole*. So whether we call the collective consciousness of all things 'God,' or simply 'the consciousness of all things,' it doesn't change the situation. The universe is sustained by an act of such stupendous and ineffable creativity that it simply cannot be reduced to such terms. Again it is a self-reference cosmology. Or as the Kalahari Bushmen so eloquently put it, 'The dream is dreaming itself.'"

From E-Squared: Nine Do-It-Yourself Energy Experiments That Prove Your Thoughts Create Your Reality *by Pam Grout*

"Quantum physics tells us that the invisible energy realm—collectively referred to as the field, or the 'FP,' as I call it—is the primary governing force of the material realm. It's the blueprint that forms reality. Indeed, we now know that the universe is made of nothing but waves and particles of energy that conform to our expectations, judgments, and beliefs. Subtle energies, thoughts, emotions, and consciousness play the starring roles in our life experiences, but because they're invisible, we haven't attempted to understand them or use them in our favor. To change the world is a simple matter of changing these expectations and beliefs. It's truly that easy. To bring something into the physical world requires focusing not on what we see, but on what we want to see."

From What the Bleep Do We Know: Discovering the Endless Possibilities for Altering Your Everyday Reality by William Arntz, Betsy Chasse, and Mark Vicente

"There have been times on this planet when humanity got together for a greater good, and the feeling of goodwill that was generated was overwhelming.

"Dr. Emoto, who has been all over the world creating coherence around the concept of water, made this observation about the Apollo 13 crisis: 'At that time, because of the spread of the TV by then, many people in the world, myself included, prayed for the safe return of the three astronauts. And that was true for even Muslim people, Christian, Buddhist, Jewish, it did not matter what religion, race or ethnicity one was. That's why I believe that such a miracle occurred.'

"During the disaster of the tsunami of Christmas 2004, a similar mass consciousness occurred. Dr. Emoto continues: We are all connected. We are entangled; if you want to call it quantum entanglement, fine. But we are entangled. And there is no real separation between us, so that what we do to another, we do to an aspect of our self. None of us are innocent in that regard. There's something out there we don't like; we can't really turn our backs on it because we're co-creators, somehow or another."

***

"I don't know about you, but those few times when humanity acted globally to help humanity, the feelings and effects were quite literally out of this world. Or rather, out of the 'more for me, mine is better than yours' world, and into a high-as-kites happy world of global-Gaia coherence. We know coherence does something. It somehow, some way pushes random quantum events around.

Coherent intent does something even more, to borrow Dr. Laszlo's words: 'It marks the full achievement of divine creativity.'"

CHAPTER 8
CASE HISTORIES OF CROWD MANIFESTING

"Creation is always happening. Every time an individual
has a thought...they're in the creation process.
Something is going to manifest out of those thoughts."
—Michael Bernard Beckwith

From The Awakened Millionaire *by Joe Vitale*

"We're victims of gas prices, gas shortages, inflation, recession, taxes, wars, and more.

"I'm going to say something unusual that may upset some people. I'm hoping it will inspire you.

"Here goes: You have more power than you think.

"While you may not want to stand in the path of war, you don't have to cower under the bed. As odd as it may sound, I believe that if enough of us think positively, we can create a counter storm of sorts. We can protect ourselves and our loved ones with our thoughts.

"I've described and proved this with the research in the back of my book *The Attractor Factor*. More than 19 studies proved that when a large group of people hold positive intentions, those intentions radiate out and become reality. I asked my readers to help stop Hurricane Rita almost 10 years ago. Rita stopped. I asked my readers to help stop the Texas wildfires several years ago. The fires stopped. I asked my readers to help my dying mother several years ago. My mother is still with us."

From Permanent Peace: How to Stop Terrorism and War—Now and Forever *by Robert Oates*

"The studies have shown that it is possible, through deliberate intervention, to end the cycle of attack and revenge—through completely peaceful means. They have defined a technology of *peace*—a systematic procedure that makes it possible to switch on peace as straightforwardly as we switch on the lights."

***

"Fortunately, this new technology has been documented nearly fifty times and confirmed in nineteen published scientific studies. Instead of objective, physical techniques, this approach uses methods that are subjective and consciousness-based—including meditation, technologies known and preserved for thousands of years in the timeless Vedic tradition of India."

***

"But if governments won't move quickly enough [to institute a plan to implement Super Radiance* meditation assemblies]—and the history of bold governmental innovation is undeniably discouraging—then peace-loving people everywhere can take the future of the world into their own hands."

Note: In this book, Oates recounts the positive results of many documented studies on using consciousness-based techniques to affect the outcome, with the cause being attributed to Super Radiance*. Some of the studies are listed below:

- Reversing a crime wave. Result: crime goes down in 24 cities.
- Reduce crime, fires, accidents, and war deaths in Israel all at once. Striking correlation between numbers of people meditating together and sum of all the variables.
- Percentage of civil cases reaching trial dropped.
- Infectious disease rate dropped.

- Infant mortality rate dropped.
- Suicide rate was the only negative variable to increase during the time period studied.
- Cigarette consumption per capita decreased.
- Alcohol consumption per capita decreased.
- Divorce rate declined.
- Traffic fatality rate declined.

From The Field: The Quest for the Secret Force of the Universe *by Lynne McTaggart*

Experiments:

"This [one of many studies recounted in the book] was as rigorous a scientific study as they come, and yet somehow their participants —all ordinary people, no psychic superstars among them—had been able to affect the random movement of machines simply by an act of will."

Discovery:

"At our essence we exist as a unity, a relationship—utterly interdependent, the parts affecting the whole at every moment."

Theory:

"Suppose you assemble an entire crowd, all focusing intently on the same thing. Would the effect be even greater? Was there a relation between the size of the crowd or the intensity of interest and the size of effect?"

Results of Crowd Studies:

"What appeared to be happening was that when attention focused the waves of individual minds on something similar, a type of group quantum 'superradiance'* occurred which had a physical effect."

"Both the type of place and the activity of the group seemed to play contributing roles in creating a kind of group consciousness."

Summary:

"We think, therefore we affect."

*Super Radiance, or superradiance, according to Oates, "comes from the superradiant effect in optical physics, in which a small proportion of coherent photons in a beam of light influences all other photons to join with them in the powerfully coherent stream that we call laser light."

Super Radiance assemblies are groups of people who, with mental focus via meditation, created the changes that were seen in the research studies, including documented global changes.

CHAPTER 9
COLLECTIVE CONSCIOUSNESS MEDITATIONS

"Consciousness is the creative element in the universe.
Without it, nothing would appear."
—Fred Alan Wolf

How and When to Think about Restoring Tibet

Any time we risk something bold and new and different, the road ahead and the outcome are not always clear to us. It often feels as if we are slogging along in an all-encompassing fog that distorts sounds and conceals our path.

We end up straining, trying hard to focus on getting through to a clearer space so we can assess our progress. It becomes stressful, and tiring. And in that exhaustion with seemingly no results in sight, it's all too easy to give up, and promise ourselves we'll try again when conditions are more favorable.

However in a mass demonstration such as this manifestation of Restoring Tibet, the fog is simply our all-pervasive disbelief in our inherent power to create.

Imagine that foggy vista is a veil that can be lifted. We lift it by gaining a better understanding of our mental abilities and the way the universal laws operate.

Your creative power is an innate ability that you were born with and have perhaps allowed to remain dormant—other than using it haphazardly and inadvertently to create the life experience you now have with its ups and downs.

That inconsistency in results is due to a lack of information about the laws of the mind that rule all creation. Whenever we lack awareness, that's actually a good situation to be in, because the solution   is to gain the awareness that's been missing. And then, with the knowledge of the steps to take and the methods to use, all you need to do is practice, and the changes will appear in ways to surprise and delight you. Usually, if not always, a big dream is preceded by signs that it is on the way. For instance, your request for more money could show up in an unexpected refund check for ten dollars. If you put yourself in a state of gratitude over that check instead of grumbling that it's not what you asked for, then you keep that door open for the rest to come to you, in perfect timing and perfect ways.

Meditation is a vital step in manifesting. Why? Because our minds are so busy every waking moment with non-stop chatter and static. During meditation, we quiet the noise, and allow in a sense of peace and calm. In this time of quietness, we open our minds to connect with spirit. That is why meditation feels rejuvenating.

For this project, Restoring Tibet, it is necessary for many minds to join together to create a new and improved collective consciousness that will affect the vibration the entire globe is in, and thus create a higher level of results.

Meditating will help you create all you desire to manifest in your own personal life, too.

In Restoring Tibet, this will not be a scene out of a corny old science fiction movie where we will each frown to demonstrate our seriousness and say the magic words "Send the Dalai Lama home" all together at a specified time, or on certain days of the week.

In fact, it is not necessary to be so precise in that timeliness of "thinking all together in the same moment," because when each participant uplifts his or her focus of thought, that means throughout the day all around the world there will be enough of a rise in the frequency on the planet to create the results we wish.

56

Our meditative thoughts will be like a benevolent wind circling the globe, and all who think of peace and love will tap into the new higher energy, and join us.

From Thought Power *by Sri Swami Sivananda*

Instead of paraphrasing and summarizing the wisdom in the pamphlet called "Thought Power," I thought it would make better reading to provide the four following excerpts, which so excellently describe what we will be doing with our thought power in the Restoring Tibet movement.

Note: "Buddha" is a title given to someone who is considered to be an "enlightened one" or "awakened one." When a mantra or teaching asks us to be Buddha-like, it is inviting us to wake up to our true spiritual nature.

"Marvels of Thought-vibrations

"Every thought that you send out is a vibration which never perishes. It goes on vibrating every particle of the universe and if your thoughts are noble, holy and forcible, they set in vibration every sympathetic mind.

"Unconsciously all people who are like you take the thought you have projected and in accordance with the capacity that they have, they send out similar thoughts. The result is that, without your knowledge of the consequences of your own work, you will be setting in motion great forces which will work together and put down the lowly and mean thoughts generated by the selfish and the wicked."

***

"Negative Thoughts Poison Life

"Thoughts of worry and thoughts of fear are fearful forces within us. They poison the very sources of life and destroy the harmony, the running efficiency, the vitality and vigour. While the opposite thoughts of cheerfulness, joy and courage, heal, soothe, instead of irritating, and immensely augment efficiency and multiply the mental powers. Be always cheerful. Smile. Laugh."

***

"Similar Thoughts Attract Each Other

"You are continually attracting towards you, from both the seen and the unseen sides of life-forces, thoughts, influences and conditions most akin to those of your own thoughts and lines."

***

"Culture the Thoughts and Become a Buddha

"Drive away from your mind all unnecessary, useless and obnoxious thoughts. Useless thoughts impede your spiritual growth; obnoxious thoughts are stumbling blocks to spiritual advancement. You are away from God when you entertain useless thoughts. Substitute thoughts of God.

"Entertain only thoughts that are helpful and useful. Useful thoughts are stepping-stones to spiritual growth and progress. Do not allow the mind to run into the old grooves and to have its own ways and habits. Be on the careful watch.

"The mental image must be of a clear-cut and well-defined thought; it must bring peace and solace to others. It should not bring even the least pain and unhappiness to anyone. Then you are a blessed soul on the earth. You are a mighty power on the earth. You can help many, heal thousands, spiritualize and elevate a large number of persons as did Jesus or Buddha."

The Heart of Manifesting a Free Tibet

Historically, we've misused the laws of the mind, only getting what we want in a hit or miss fashion, out of ignorance of the right techniques. This is despite their availability in secret messages of ancient texts such as Biblical metaphors that have been misunderstood and taken literally instead of metaphysically. Because of this, it's necessary for us to do some tweaking about our beliefs.

When we believe something is impossible, it remains impossible. Meditation will help us collectively reach that state of belief that we have all the creative power we need to manifest Restoring Tibet. In a contemplative or meditative state, we connect with our higher selves and tap into Source, God, the One Mind that creates everything.

One positive thought neutralizes many thousands of negative ones because positivity is at a higher, finer frequency and is more condensed in its power, while negativity has a low, dense, fear-based vibration.

For instance, when we allow ourselves to be afraid (even terrified) that a certain political candidate will win, our fear makes his campaign more powerful. How could this be? Because our fear means we are vibrating in harmony with his agenda.

We the Peaceful have more power than we realize, and we haven't been using it to create the change we want to see.

We've been using it to push against those with agendas of hate, building walls and greed—and that pushing against simply feeds power into that other agenda.

We MUST turn the other cheek—that means to turn our attention away from what we don't want and towards what we do want.

It sounds simple and we nod when we hear this, but why aren't we doing it?

Let's put into action all that we've learned in movies like *The Shift, The Moses Code,* and *The Secret*, in books about manifesting, in seminars and workshops and home study programs.

You don't have to go anywhere special.

You don't need to take a lot of time out of your busy day.

You don't need to wait for an event, or seminar, or someone to tell you to start.

And you don't need to learn or memorize complicated instructions of any kind.

It's simple.

1) At least once a day, take a Time Out. Relax your shoulders, breathe mindfully, and use the 15-minute meditation called "Meditation for Restoring Tibet."

2) Throughout the day, get in the habit of noticing how you are feeling. As needed, do what it takes to get your mood up into the Happy Zone.

Dance, listen to upbeat music, play with your pet or your children, repeat an affirmation that feels good to you.

Understand that you are the only one who can think your thoughts and feel your feelings and make your choices. It sounds obvious, but we've been trained since early childhood to look to others to do all this for us, because we've also been taught that we are pretty much powerless.

Claim your power today. The meditations will help.

Choose happiness today, and lighten up your energy frequency.

3) Optional: use the 3-minute meditation "At the Potala Palace" in addition to the 15-minute meditation.

4) You'll find free audio and video meditations at RestoringTibet. com/book-meditations

5) Additional material to support your desires is available in my blog articles in the "Notes" tab and motivational quotations at Facebook. com/RestoringTibet That's also the place to find updates about the project and event announcements.

15-Minute Meditation—the Core of This Project

Introduction:
Whether we expect good or bad things to happen in life, the power of our expectation (aligned with our belief) predicts our results.

To change the results, we need to change our predictions.

In this meditation, we will use the collective consciousness as it is intended to be used: to create global expansion, more love and more peace and more joy.

Take a few moments to prepare your body and mind to meditate. You don't have to do anything special such as lighting candles or incense, but do whatever you enjoy and make this a personal experience for yourself. If you tend to drift into sleep if you lie down to meditate, please do this meditation in a seated position with your back supported if that is more comfortable for you.

Breathe in slowly and deeply, and let yourself relax fully as you exhale. Do this a few times, and then allow your natural breathing rhythm to take over. Wriggle your shoulders and rotate your neck to ease any tension that has built up.

Ready? Gently dismiss mind chatter as it pops up, trying to get your attention. Tune out distractions, and allow yourself to go on this journey with me:

Meditation for Restoring Tibet

Begin by remembering that you are an eternal spirit with all the powers of creation that you desire and require to manifest change in the world and in your own life.

Breathe in this special awareness. No need to count your breaths or wait for an instruction to inhale and exhale, simply breathe naturally, and follow along with the imagery.

Allow yourself to let thoughts of the outside world and your everyday activities to drift out of sight as if carried away on the gentle breeze, and do not call them back to you. Gently dismiss distractions with the silent promise to pay attention to them later, if needed. Trust that you will easily remember anything important when you are finished meditating.

Inhale slowly, imagining that the air you draw in from the physical world you inhabit is imbued with love, happiness and kindness. These invisible, precious feelings fill you with the joy of expectation.

Something good is about to happen, and you are eager for it to manifest.

Exhale, blowing out all the resistance, anxiety and fear that have created a dark cloud in your heart.

Inhale joy. Feel it saturate every cell of your body with bliss and alignment.

Exhale the sludge of resistance, blowing it out with a forceful exhalation to clear it away. The dark sludge dissolves into harmless white light, and can't touch you anymore.

Fearful thoughts have no substance. They are all illusions, and cannot harm you unless you use fear as the launching platform for your daily manifestations.

Continue breathing calmly, slowly, deeply. Allow your own easy rhythm to take over the operation of breathing.

Imagine you are on a sparkling private beach, or in a serene garden, or on a pristine mountaintop, on the most perfect day. Everything about this adventure delights you. Stroll around, or sit comfortably and enjoy the view.

Experience the abiding sense of peace and contentment. You feel happy and centered, for no particular reason—just because you are at ease being alone with yourself.

Take this opportunity to reflect on your life journey and notice places where you would like to amplify the love so that it goes deeper and broader.

Recognize there are things in life that you would like to do that you are not doing yet. Breathe in the awareness that you have the power to create what you desire, and you have access to everything you need.

Let go of any feelings of doubt, release any sense of discouragement about past situations where you wanted to manifest love or health or prosperity for yourself and others, but it didn't happen the way you wanted.

Understand you are not to blame. You were simply acting under old rules that do not work and never have. Most of the world still follows those rules, but you no longer have to remain in thrall to them. Now that you have the correct instructions, manifesting a life you love will be easier and more delightful.

During this joy amplification process, you may discover hidden promises and forgotten agreements you made with your higher self before you were born. Release regret that you did not make this discovery sooner, and understand that you are right where you need to be today to fulfill your life purpose. If you feel a sense of regret that you don't have enough time to make up for past neglect, remember that God makes a way where there seemingly is no way.

Call on the Spirit of Light to fill you, allowing the beautiful light to swirl down into the crown of your head and drench your entire body. The light uplifts and energizes you as your physical nature blends with your higher self and All that Is.

Take a moment now to create your intention. Perhaps it is to keep evolving upward into more love and joy. You have the power to manifest all you want, including helping to send the Dalai Lama home to Tibet. Think about all the other things in life that you would enjoy experiencing: improved health, more money, happier and more loving relationships, a higher level of self-expression and service to the world.

The path of service allows growth and expansion while it fills your days with joy and contentment. Make your intention now, state it out loud if you wish, and claim it for yourself.

This is real. This is really happening. You are creating the reality you desire, a reality of more peace and understanding in the world because of your willingness to lift your thoughts to a higher and finer vibration than the everyday habits of common hour thinking.

Now turn your attention to what you want for others. If there is someone in your life you would like to help, or people you have heard about whose situation evokes compassion, think of these people now, including the Dalai Lama and Tibetan refugees. Bring to mind a better outcome for them and relief from their present circumstances.

Ask your higher self to work with their higher selves to create this joyful blend of loving thoughts. Imagine they have all that they want. Imagine how good they will feel and how grateful you feel already, knowing you have helped uplift them out of their present situation into a better one.

Create a bright and pure picture of their happiness and relief. Let the light of love fill you with a benevolent glow that radiates out from you towards everyone else in the world.

Now that you have stated your intention, you feel a sense of growing anticipation. Something wonderful is on the way. Its arrival is a sure thing, not a mere wish. Relax in the knowledge that from now on, everything always turns out beautifully for you. Release any and all regrets for the past. Forgive everyone including yourself for mistakes made. Claim your power to purposefully create this life in ways that expand your joy.

Breathe in the delicious awareness that you are changing your own life and the lives of others by your deliberate attention to using the power of your thoughts in this focused meditation.

Your thoughts are like boomerangs. They always come back to you, bringing the matching results into your life, as if you had sent out a message with an order and the delivery person came to your door with exactly what you asked for.

The secret to getting what you want is to be careful with that boomerang. Think, feel and act in congruence with love, compassion and kindness, and then your boomerang will zoom back to you with everything on that same harmonious wavelength.

Make a new habit of releasing old beliefs that weaken you with feelings of unworthiness, or the idea that the only path to success is struggle and hard work.

Repeat these words: Whatever I visualize for others, I receive in my own life, too. When I imagine peace for others, I receive and experience peace in my own life. Each time I picture freedom for Tibet, I have more freedom in my own life.

When you open your awareness to the light and the power of creation, you open the door to the promised land of all you desire and long to achieve.

There is no need to push away your old beliefs about struggle and lack. Force makes those beliefs grow stronger. Instead, open your mind to the vision of what you want, such as more joy, and contemplate what it would feel like to experience joy at a higher degree. Vigorous health, financial freedom, a loving marriage or partnership, joyful family interactions, fulfilling self-expression. All of this and more is within your reach.

Bring to mind the best qualities you want people around you to have, and then commit to only seeing those qualities from now on. When their behavior is not in alignment with the qualities you enjoy, simply ignore it and continue to evoke what you do want from the relationship. Soon, they will not behave in that other way around you, because you are not a match for it. Make sure you are the embodiment of the fine qualities you want each person in your life to have. As the Dalai Lama teaches, be loving, kind, and compassionate. This life philosophy creates a harmonious vibration to attract the same-natured experiences right back to you.

Take a moment now to reflect on how good it feels to be part of the biggest peaceful manifestation in history. When you said "Yes" to participating in this movement, you immediately put yourself in harmonious vibration with the intention of Restoring Tibet. You added your voice and your invisible thought waves to the global consciousness of humanity, in a positive wavelength that has the power to uplift the masses out of the old worldview of war, destruction and poverty, and into the new worldview of peace, compassion and respect, food, housing and education for all, loving acceptance of diversity, and the toppling of walls and fences.

Realize that you are not the same person you were at the beginning of this journey within. You have tapped into a higher level of yourself, and with that connection, you will experience improved results in your everyday life from now on. Each time you enter this meditation, you reach a higher level of awareness and you come away from it with a deepened sense of connection with Spirit and with all other beings.

Trust that what you are doing always makes a difference in the world. Your words and thoughts have impact, and it is up to you whether you choose a positive or harmful path.

With faith in your own spiritual nature and your ability to co-create with Source, you continue to grow and expand, and in response to this expansion, all the prosperity, love and joy you desire now comes into your life, the perfect match to your improved energy and finer vibration.

Come back into awareness now of your surroundings. You can revisit your walk on the beach or in the garden or on the mountaintop to refresh and reinvigorate at any time. Simply close your eyes for a moment, visualize yourself there and capture the feelings of peace, joy and expansion that you experienced earlier. Please take a moment now to visualize the Dalai Lama enjoying his own peaceful walks along the lake outside the Potala Palace with a vista of the mountains and gardens in free Tibet.

The journey home is sweet.

3-Minute Meditation ("At the Potala Palace")

I wrote this meditation on 3/4/16, a few weeks after getting the idea for Restoring Tibet, and began using the audio MP3 twice a day to immerse myself in the vision of the Dalai Lama at home once again, at the Potala Palace in Lhasa, Tibet. I still use this meditation twice daily. It is short and sweet, but the imagery has the power to create change.

I created a video version of this meditation for you, using my spoken meditation as the audio track. The music is "Just like Heaven" by Jeff Woodall, used with permission.

You'll find the free audio and video meditations at RestoringTibet. com/book-meditations

Before you begin reading the meditation below, take a few moments to relax your shoulders and calm your breathing. Imagine closing your eyes, as you'll be able to do when you use the audio/video versions.

Tune out distractions and allow yourself to go on this journey with me:

Meditation to Envision the Dalai Lama at Home in Tibet

I command my body to relax, and it does so instantly. I now open my imagination to envision events in the near future, and then to bring these events into the present with the power of focused manifestation.

Closing my eyes, I see the magnificent, ancient Potala Palace in Lhasa, Tibet. I go inside and start looking around. I discover the Dalai Lama, meditating in a small hidden courtyard. I sit quietly near him and bask in the peace and serenity.

I sense his heart expanding in gratitude for all life and blessings for humanity, and I feel called to express more love, more joy, more compassion in my own life.

He continues to meditate, and so I decide to explore the vast Palace. I pass people who are peering into shrine areas, and I pass monks who are meditating or studying. I see areas of restoration, of places being readied for ancient works of Tibetan art to be returned.

I hear music that feels familiar, as if I've known it all my life. I begin humming spontaneously. The sound of my soul blends with the music and I realize the wordless song is a request circling the globe, asking people to return ancient documents, statues, paintings, and historical artifacts to their rightful place at the Palace.

Returning to the hidden courtyard, I arrive in time to see the Dalai Lama end his meditation. He smiles and greets me by name. I bow my head and ask for his blessing. He places a hand on my shoulder, tilts my chin up, and looks deep into my eyes. We share a silent moment of pure love and appreciation for life and All That Is.

Then he throws back his head and laughs in joy as he waves a hand around at the palace and thanks me for helping to bring him home. Then, with another laugh, he reminds me that we are always at home, wherever we are.

We go outside the Palace together, where a massive crowd of Tibetans and people from around the world are waiting for him. He extends his blessing of love, kindness and compassion.

When he finishes speaking, I say to him, "Thank you for this special visit with you, Your Holiness. I am grateful I have been guided to be part of your return to Tibet."

Namaste.

CHAPTER 10
ADD YOUR VOICE TO THE JOURNEY HOME

"Time is a created thing. To say 'I don't have time,'
is like saying, 'I don't want to.'"
—Lao Tzu

At the heart of every project are the action steps that are necessary to bring the dream into fulfillment. Without action, any wish remains simply a wish, and never a reality.

For Individuals

1. Commit to the daily meditation practice described in Chapter 9.
2. Add more meditation time as desired.
3. Share the project with your friends, and invite them to join in.
4. Follow Restoring Tibet in social media.
5. Attend upcoming events—look for updates at facebook.com/restoringtibet

For Bloggers

In addition to "For Individuals," please consider:

Write a blog post about Restoring Tibet—permission is granted to quote up to 500 words from this book if authorship is correctly attributed according to the copyright.

For Authors, Motivational Speakers and Coaches

In addition to "For Individuals," please consider:

Affiliate and speaker opportunities will be available as the project grows. Stay tuned at facebook.com/restoringtibet for details on where to sign up.

For Thought Leaders

In addition to "For Individuals," please consider:

Contact your subscribers about the Restoring Tibet project, and ask them to "like" the project's page at facebook.com/restoringtibet

Get involved in the growth of this movement. I'm counting on you to step up and help me bring the Dalai Lama home.

For School Teachers

In addition to "For Individuals," please consider:

In social studies class, or for a special cultural project, turn your attention toward Tibetans and their rich history of tapestries, mantra flags, prayer wheels, singing bowls, art, music and dance.

The children could create a play about the celestial "Tibetan Snow Lion." Prior to 1959, the Snow lion was the national emblem of Tibet. Tibetan Snow Lion dances are still performed, in India.

*Bumper Sticker Game – a word game for children of all ages.

*Mirror Mantras (backwards printing, needs to be read in a mirror or by clever students who can figure it out!)

[*See the end of this book for black and white images; go to restoringtibet.com/book-posters for color images you can download. Please share in social media.]

For Community In luencers

In addition to "For Individuals," please consider:

Speak out in favor of a free Tibet. This book is not promoting a political agenda, however, as a person who experiences freedom in your own community, you can help spread the news about Restoring Tibet.

For Tibetan Organizations

In addition to "For Individuals," please consider:

I welcome your participation in Restoring Tibet. Please contact the author at evelynbrooks.com if you wish to discuss ways we can facilitate this project. I am open to suggestions and ideas for collaborating.

GLOBAL EVENTS & HAPPENINGS

"You can achieve your destiny by using your creativity
and your positive emotions, because feeling any
one such emotion will attract events, people,
circumstances and outcomes that resonate to its vibration."
—Peggy McColl

As part of this "Global Action Plan to Send the 14th Dalai Lama Home," I submit the following ideas. Please note that as of the date of this book's publication, 9/11/16, these are "wish list" items:

Live & Televised Events

- Live events! Tickets to attend in person would be sold to cover expenses and create a fund for the no-cost events. The membership area online [see below] would have the event available to view streaming on the Dalai Lama's new online channel at the project's website. Perhaps there would be a fee to watch the replay. The point is to make the powerful live events readily available because in the collective viewing, we access the power of our collective consciousness to create the new reality we desire: the restoring of Tibet, and the manifestation of love, peace, kindness and compassion throughout the world.

- IMAGINE this: Concerts televised worldwide, featuring entertainers from around the world, leading us in energetic songs to get everyone's vibration flying high...and centered around the intention to IMAGINE the Dalai Lama living in Tibet — throughout, a video montage would show the Dalai Lama walking the streets of Lhasa, surrounded by Tibetans, going about normal everyday life in Tibet, being interviewed outside the Potala Palace, strolling the palace interior, all with location captions to embed the message: <u>He is home again.</u>

The goal is not to excite ourselves with a "hope" or a "wish" that somehow the Dalai Lama will be magically transported from India to Tibet, but to instill a firm belief in each heart that he is already in the process of returning home. And, of course, there'd be a gigantic singalong of "Imagine" to end the event. T-shirts: *You may say I'm a dreamer, but I'm not the only one. We're sending the Dalai Lama home.*

- Envision this televised live event: A vast amphitheater overflowing with tens of thousands of people. Speakers such as Dr. Hew Len, Dr. Joe Vitale, Mabel Katz, a representative of Morrnah Simeona (1913-1992, founder of Self I-dentity through Ho'oponopono), and other Ho'oponopono experts would explain the history and the power of Ho'oponopono. Hawaiian singers lead us in a song: *Ho'oponopono... I'm sorry... Please forgive me...Thank you... I love you...* The words appear on screens in different languages so everyone around the world can participate—we could have a lottery among the participants to pick someone to be on stage for each of the major languages the project offers in its material, so that the event is truly global as we sing in the world's major languages. We easily create a very high global vibration of forgiveness and love. Strangers hug, hold hands, express tears of joy at what we are manifesting together! Hawaiian dancers— starting with little children—fill the stage. A massive Tibetan Snow Lion (two dancers in a costume, representing Tibet's beloved emblem) wearing a hula skirt bounds on stage–her antics with the children delight viewers and the high frequency of laughter encircles the globe. Tibetan dancers join the performers. Thousands dance at their seats and in the aisles and at home.

The Dalai Lama appears on a huge video screen to thank us and give us his blessing. Or, perhaps, we have planned a surprise for the audience and television viewers: ornate screens at the back of the stage slide away, revealing the Dalai Lama seated on a raised platform. Chinese acrobats and Bollywood dancers glide it forward and the entertainment goes on around His Holiness before he speaks.

The finale: brilliant, rousing music and fireworks or a light show, depending on the venue.

- Picture this: an amazing live concert with famous singers and bands (all donating their time for the Dalai Lama's return to Tibet). When Pharrell Williams sings his famous song "Happy," dancers perform on stilts — *"My love is too high, can't nothing bring me down!"*

- Invite corporate sponsors to promote the different events and provide gifts to participants or for special drawings to win prizes.

Meditation Club

- "The Daily Dalai" — brief meditation video every day, featuring the Dalai Lama with well-known speakers/teachers about the Law of Attraction and related topics, discussing an idea or quote to inspire participants to uplift to higher levels of thinking rather than reacting to the logic of "conditions" they can see.

- Daily emails to participants, containing a written affirmation and a meditation MP3 to enjoy and to share in social media. All MP3s would be posted in the membership area for easy access.

- Mobile app for free guided meditations and other free content plus in-app purchases of additional related content.

Membership Site (free and paid levels)

- The membership website will be the central place to go for links to attend live streaming and online events or watch the videos and replays, enjoy a video training series about how to use the laws of the mind to participate more fully in this project of returning the Dalai Lama to Tibet, access the meditation series and MP3s that go out daily, claim their downloadable gifts, etc.

- For-a-fee membership could include access to a higher level of gifts from project affiliates in the personal development field, plus coaching lessons on using the laws of the mind to get what you want in life. The more people who understand how to use the laws, the more smooth, easy and swift will be the Dalai Lama's return to Tibet.

- The private members area could include the Dalai Lama's new TV channel online, to access video messages from the Dalai Lama as well as guest speakers.

- Affiliates and Sponsors would be invited to provide gifts such as MP3s, affirmations, e-books, videos, etc. that are supportive of manifesting the Dalai Lama's return while helping everyone in their own personal development and greater understanding of the mental laws. At least some gifts should be available in multiple languages. Some material could be printable, to share with friends and family, particularly in areas of the world where many people who would support this project might not have online access.

- Participants would be invited to write a goal card to be read twice a day: *I am so happy and grateful now that the Dalai Lama is home again in Tibet and all is well!*

- In the membership area online, participants would be invited to share their MEMORIES of the successfully completed event–in advance! This technique will access the power of "the wish fulfilled" by showing people how to look into the future and then imagine they are REMEMBERING what the event was like for them in detail. This could include making new friends in the membership area, attending an online or live event, memories of how great it felt to understand how to use the law of attraction to improve their own lives in a certain way such as getting a promotion at work, traveling to Tibet to be there for the big celebration welcoming the Dalai Lama home. Perhaps members would be able to "like" their favorite shares, and then the most "liked" shares would be included in a book after the event with all these wonderful memories-from-the-future whose vibration helped create the end result.

Online Happenings

- Love-ins and Happenings! The O'Jays "Love Train" could be at the center of an ongoing online event–members of The O'Jays have changed over the years but are still performing and would be a great addition to the project. "People all over the world, join in! Start a love train, love train!... The next stop that we make will be England...." And we'll change that to: "The next stop that we make will be ... LHASA!"

- "Today I Am a Tibetan" video contest — amateurs only. Individuals and groups (such as clubs or school classes) would submit their video related to Tibet, including its history, with the rule that it must be positive in nature to be considered. (Example: a traditional Tibetan dance, or a play with the Tibetan Snow Lion as a central character.) Semi-finalists will be selected by a panel, and then membership votes will determine the winners. Prizes to be donated by event sponsors.

- Global Peace Happenings—blog talk radio events to share the love.

- Videos of flash mob events with upbeat songs, joyfully celebrating in advance His Holiness's return to Tibet.

Webinars

- EFT (Emotional Freedom Technique) tapping experts would teach listeners/viewers to release doubt and open the in-flow of desired results — both within the project and in their own lives.

- Guest speakers could be interviewed on various topics to discuss how to manifest what you want in life, as well as manifesting the Dalai Lama's return to Tibet.

Online Marketplace

- Invite affiliates to share the project with their lists and invite their followers to sign up for either the free or paid membership.

- Marketplace in the membership area: affiliates may offer their digital programs (such as e-courses on the Law of Attraction, meditation video series, etc.) and downloadable products for sale. All affiliates are vetted first, to be sure their work in the world is in alignment with the high spiritual nature of "Restoring Tibet."

- Online store open to the public and to all members (for-a-fee membership level would include a store discount): official "Restoring Tibet" merchandise would be offered for sale, such as t-shirts, hats, mugs, buttons, and downloadable MP3 collections that are exclusive at this site.

Sponsorships for Returning Tibetan Refugees

- Assist qualifying native Tibetans/descendants to return to Tibet from Dharamsala by soliciting donations from participants and others, to pay all or part of the cost of relocating an individual or family.

- A portion of each sale in the website marketplace could go to a non-profit organization funding the return to Tibet.

INVOCATION, PRAYERS AND AFFIRMINGS

Note: Posters for some of the following affirmations and prayers can be viewed in the next section, Restoring Tibet—Posters, and are also available to share in social media and download at RestoringTibet. com/book-posters.

Spiritual Freedom

I was raised Catholic and I still have a beautiful old rosary with wooden beads. If I wanted to, I could walk down any street in most (not all, yet) countries of the world and pray out loud with those beads in full view of everyone, even the police. I might get a few curious looks, but I wouldn't be risking arrest, or torture, or threat of death.

That ordinary example of spiritual self-expression and freedom of speech that so many of us take for granted has been denied to those Tibetans who remain in their homeland.

Invocation

"God Bless Us Everyone"

(by Alan Silvestri and Glenn Ballard,
from the film *A Christmas Carol)*

Come together one and all
In the giving spirit
Gifts abound here great and small
Joyously we feel it

Blessings sent us from above

Guide us on our way
We raise our voice as we rejoice
Bow our head and pray

A miracle has just begun
God bless us everyone

To the voices no one hears
We have come to find you
With your laughter and your tears
Goodness, hope and virtue

Father, mother, daughter, son
Each a treasure be
One candle's light dispels the night
Now our eyes can see

Burning brighter than the sun
God bless us everyone

A miracle has just begun
God bless us everyone

Prayers and Mantras

Traditional Tibetan Chant

Om Mani Padme Hum

Tibetan Buddhists believe that saying *Om Mani Padme Hum* many times a day, either out loud or silently, will invoke the blessings of Chenrezig, who is the embodiment of compassion. It is considered the most beneficial, powerful, and purifying mantra. Traditionally, the words are carved on rocks, and also written on papers that are then inserted into prayer wheels.

NOTE: According to a *Time* magazine article about the Dalai Lama dated March 17, 2015, "Tibetans can still be arrested if caught with the writings or a picture of the Buddhist leader and recipient of the 1989 Nobel Peace Prize."

The following explanation of this six-syllable mantra is excerpted from the transcript of a lecture given in New Jersey by the Dalai Lama, which can be read in full at: The Meaning of Om Mani Padme Hum [URL: sacred-texts.com/bud/tib/omph.htm]

"It is very good to recite the mantra OM MANI PADME HUM, but while you are doing it, you should be thinking on its meaning, for the meaning of the six syllables is great and vast. The first, OM, is composed of three pure letters, A, U, and M. These symbolize the practitioner's impure body, speech, and mind; they also symbolize the pure exalted body, speech and mind of a Buddha....

"The path is indicated by the next four syllables. MANI, meaning jewel.... Just as a jewel is capable of removing poverty, so the altruistic mind of enlightenment is capable of removing the poverty, or difficulties, of cyclic existence and of solitary peace.... [and] PADME, meaning lotus, symbolizes wisdom....

"Purity must be achieved by an indivisible unity of method and wisdom, symbolized by the final syllable, HUM, which indicates indivisibility....

"Thus the six syllables, OM MANI PADME HUM, mean that in dependence on the practice which is an indivisible union of method and wisdom, you can transform your impure body, speech and mind into the pure body, speech, and mind of a Buddha."

Dhan Dhan Ram Daas Gur for Miracles

"Dhan Dhan Ram Das Gur is the ultimate prayer of miracles. It will make the impossible possible in your life. Those who work with it will experience the help and grace of Heaven. Through a devotional practice Dhan Dhan Ram Das Gur will invoke perfect extraordinary occurrences, better known as miracles. It is a mighty prayer of limitless blessings. If you or your loved ones are in dire need, devote yourself to this Naam. It gives hope where there is no hope and causes Grace to come through for you." Dr. Michael Joseph Levry

Dhan Dhan Ram Daas Gur jin siriaa tinai savareya

Poorey hoee karamaath aap sirjanharai dhareya

Sikhi athei sangati parbrahm kar namaskareya

Atal athahu atol thoo thera anth na paravareya

Jiney thoo seveya bhao kar sae thud paar outareya

Laab lobh kaam karodh mohu maar kadeh thud saparvareya

Dhan so therah than hai sach terah paisarkaariaa

Nanak thoo, Lehna thoohai Gur Amar thoo vichareya

Gur Dhitha thaa maan saadhareya

The Twenty-Third Psalm

(A Psalm of David; for miracles, healing, and Divine intercession) *The*

Lord (Law) is my shepherd; I shall not want.

He maketh me to lie down in green pastures: he leadeth me beside the still waters.

He restoreth my soul: he leadeth me in the paths of righteousness for his name's sake.

Yea, though I walk through the valley of the shadow of death, I will

fear no evil: for thou art with me; thy rod and thy staff they comfort me.

Thou preparest a table before me in the presence of mine enemies: thou anointest my head with oil; my cup runneth over.

Surely goodness and mercy shall follow me all the days of my life: and I will dwell in the house of the Lord forever.

21-Beads Prayer or Mantra

(by Evelyn Brooks)

Before you begin, notice that in this prayer we invoke compassion for those whom the Dalai Lama calls our "sacred friends"—these are the people, governments and organizations whom it would be all too easy to hate, but instead we look for the lessons they can teach us to grow in our own awareness and lift ourselves up and out of the reactions that lead to unrest and agitation in our own hearts.

I am grateful the Dalai Lama is home in Tibet

May I be happy
May I be peaceful
May I be free
May I be loving
May I radiate joy

May my friends be happy
May my friends be peaceful
May my friends be free
May my friends be loving
May my friends radiate joy

May my sacred friends be happy
May my sacred friends be peaceful

May my sacred friends be free
May my sacred friends be loving
May my sacred friends radiate joy

May all events be happy
May all events be peaceful
May all events be free
May all events be loving
May all events radiate joy

Healing the Past with Ho 'oponopono

From *Zero Limits* by Dr. Joe Vitale and Dr. Hew Len:

Simply put, Ho'oponopono means, "to make right" or "to rectify an error."

Ho'o means "cause" in Hawaiian and *ponopono* means "perfection."

Ho'oponopono is a problem-solving process. But it's done entirely within yourself.

When you do Ho'oponopono, the Divinity takes the painful situation and neutralizes or purifies it.

The Basic 4-Step Ho'oponopono Healing Practice

Say these 4 phrases until you feel clear and at peace:

I love you

I'm sorry

Please forgive me

Thank you

Affirmings

Whatever we affirm, good or bad, is what we create in life. Let's begin to affirm goodness, compassion, kindness, love and peace.

Affirm now:

It feels so good to imagine the Dalai Lama at home in Tibet.

This is a cool project. I'm happy to be part of returning the Dalai Lama home.

Now I'm doing this, I know how to manifest more good in my own life.

I tap into a higher awareness that I create my own reality.

I agree with the Dalai Lama's message of kindness and compassion.

I know I can focus my thoughts and achieve what I want.

I believe I can and do make a difference.

I am grateful for all the blessings in my life.

I radiate light and joy wherever I go.

Florence Scovel Shinn, from a 1936 manuscript

"If you hate and resent a situation, you have fastened it to yourself, for you attract what you fear or dislike....

"History will repeat itself until you think you are cursed with misfortune and injustice.

"There is only one way to neutralize it. Be absolutely undisturbed by the injustice, and send goodwill to all concerned.

"**Affirm: My goodwill is a strong Tower around me. I now change all enemies into friends. All inharmony into harmony. All injustice into justice.**"

RESTORING TIBET — POSTERS

"Fear is excitement without the breath.
Here's what this intriguing statement means: the very same
mechanisms that produce excitement also produce fear, and any
fear can be transformed into excitement by breathing
fully with it."
—Gay Hendricks

You can find all of these posters (and any new additions after this
book is released on 9/11/16) at RestoringTibet.com/book-posters

Restoring Tibet: The Project One-Page

PROJECT: "RESTORING TIBET"
                  SEND THE 14th DALAI LAMA HOME

STATEMENT OF INTENTION: By meditating together globally, we will manifest a new reality in which the Dalai Lama returns to a free Tibet.

WHAT IT IS: The biggest peaceful manifestation in history.

"Whatever the mind can conceive and believe, it can achieve."
   – Napoleon Hill

Where will participants come from?
Answer: From personal development and spiritual growth communities, friends of Tibet, and the Dalai Lama's followers.

See below--one of the Dalai Lama's Facebook accounts has 13+ million likes.

- By combining our magnetic powers of manifestation, we will bring forth, from out of the field of infinite possibilities, the Dalai Lama's return to Tibet as its spiritual leader.
- We will collectively create the biggest positive demonstration in history. (Up until now the biggest demonstrations have been World War 1 and World War 2.)
- We will join globally in meditations and joyful events to celebrate and focus on the Dalai Lama's return to Tibet.
- We will bring His Holiness home by visualizing he is already there, and then allowing the law of attraction to open up opportunities to take as the project unfolds.

Visit RestoringTibet.com to learn more

WHAT COULD YOU DO TODAY IF YOU DIDN'T THINK THIS WAS IMPOSSIBLE?

contact

Evelyn Brooks
Facebook.com/RestoringTibet

To: His Holiness
The Dalai Lama

Happy Birthday
July 6, 2016
Next year in Tibet!

RestoringTibet.com
A Global Peace Manifestation

xox Evelyn Roberts Brooks
ADD YOUR NAME TO THE CARD BY SHARING

I AM the happy manifestor who helped bring the Dalai Lama home to Tibet.

Change Injustice to Justice

If you hate and resent a situation, you have fastened it to yourself, for you attract what you fear or dislike....

History will repeat itself until you think you are cursed with misfortune and injustice.

There is only one way to neutralize it. Be absolutely undisturbed by the injustice, and send goodwill to all concerned.

Affirm: **My goodwill is a strong Tower around me. I now change all enemies into friends. All inharmony into harmony. All injustice into justice.**

Florence Scovel Shinn, 1936 manuscript

RestoringTibet.com

Experiments with the Collective Consciousness

The Collective Consciousness
(notes from *The Field** by Lynne McTaggart)

Experiments:

"This [one of many studies recounted in the book] was as rigorous a scientific study as they come, and yet somehow their participants -- all ordinary people, no psychic superstars among them -- had been able to affect the random movement of machines simply by an act of will."

Discovery:

"At our essence we exist as a unity, a relationship -- utterly interdependent, the parts affecting the whole at every moment."

Theory:

"Suppose you assemble an entire crowd, all focusing intently on the same thing. Would the effect be even greater? Was there a relation between the size of the crowd or the intensity of interest and the size of effect?"

Results of Crowd Studies:

"What appeared to be happening was that when attention focused the waves of individual minds on something similar, a type of group quantum 'superradiance' occurred which had a physical effect."

"Both the type of place and the activity of the group seemed to play contributing roles in creating a kind of group consciousness."

RestoringTibet.com

"We think, therefore we affect."
*THE FIELD: The Quest for the Secret Force of the Universe

Operation of Your Mental Picture

"Operation of Your Mental Picture"

"All you have to do
is to make such a mental picture
of your heart's desire,
and hold it cheerfully in place
with your will,
always conscious that the same
Infinite Power which
brought the universe into existence
brought you into form
for the purpose of enjoying
Itself in and through you.
And since it is all Life, Love, Light,
Power, Peace, Beauty, and Joy,
and is the only Creative Power there is,
the form it takes in and through you depends
upon the direction given it by your thought."

Genevieve Behrend, from _Your Invisible Power_ (1929)

RestoringTibet.com

21-Beads Prayer or Mantra

I am grateful the Dalai Lama is home in Tibet
May I be happy
May I be peaceful
May I be free
May I be loving
May I radiate joy
May my friends be happy
May my friends be peaceful
May my friends be free
May my friends be loving
May my friends radiate joy
May my sacred friends be happy
May my sacred friends be peaceful
May my sacred friends be free
May my sacred friends be loving
May my sacred friends radiate joy
May all events be happy
May all events be peaceful
May all events be free
May all events be loving
May all events radiate joy

RestoringTibet.com

Healing the Past with Ho'oponopono

Healing the Past with Ho'oponopono

Simply put, Ho'oponopono means, 'to make right' or 'to rectify an error.'

Ho'o means 'cause' in Hawaiian and ponopono means 'perfection.'

Ho'oponopono is a problem-solving process. But it's done entirely within yourself.

When you do Ho'oponopono, the Divinity takes the painful situation and neutralizes or purifies it.

Dr. Joe Vitale & Dr. Hew Len, _Zero Limits_

The Basic 4-Step Ho'oponopono Healing Practice. Say these 4 phrases until you feel clear and at peace:

I love you

I'm sorry

Please forgive me

Thank you

RestoringTibet.com

Affirmations to Support the Journey Home

"The Dalai Lama's Journey Home"

It feels so good	This is a cool project.	Now I'm doing this
Feels Good	**Cool Project**	**I Know How**
to imagine the Dalai Lama at home in Tibet.	I'm happy to be part of returning the Dalai Lama home.	I know how to manifest more good in my own life.
I tap into	I agree with	I know I can
Create	**Kindness**	**Focus**
a higher awareness that I create my own reality.	the Dalai Lama's message of kindness and compassion.	focus my thoughts and achieve what I want.
I believe I can and do	I am grateful	I radiate
I Believe	**Grateful**	**Joy**
make a difference.	for all the blessings in my life.	light and joy wherever I go.

RestoringTibet.com
Sending the Dalai Lama Home

How to Do It and Where the Money Will Come From

"If you can see it then you can do it. How are you going to do it? Well, you'll be able to tell the person that *after* you do it. It's not all locked up in your intellect. It's locked up in faith. It's locked up in the belief that if you hold the idea in your mind, you'll move into the vibration that will attract it.

"That's why you've got to understand the laws. You've got to understand your relationship to the laws. And you've got to know that you can do it. Where will the money come from? Wherever it is right now! You will attract it."

Bob Proctor

The 4-Word (Forward) Bumper Sticker Game

The 4-Word (Forward) Bumper Sticker Game

Imagine you are in a caravan of cars, bikes and buses going to a concert and light festival to celebrate the Dalai Lama's return to Tibet as its spiritual leader.

Your goal: create as many 4-word bumper stickers as you can. Imagine you see a blank bumper sticker ahead of you. Fill in the 4 words to create a statement, affirmation or intention.

Rules:
- 4 words exactly
- Family-friendly
- Upbeat
- Avoid negative words, including contractions such as "can't," "don't," "won't," etc. Example: please up-spin "We can't lose now" to "We are winning now"
- Do use contractions and hyphens to reduce the # of words. (I'm, he's, she's, let's, who'll, where'll, well-being, etc.)
- Punctuation and symbols are not included in your word count. Express yourself!!!
- Have fun! Silly alliterations and puns are welcome. This is a <u>game</u>, not a grammar lesson.

Ready? Let's get started!

Dalai Lama is home ♥	I love feeling good	_____
Whoo-hoo if you're happy!	Laughter heals all boo-boos	_____
I always spiral upward	There is One Mind	_____
There's another happy manifestor!	We are all connected	_____
Everything is working out	Let the healing begin	_____
Life's an incredible journey	Joy sticks to me	_____
I forgive everyone now	I am always soul-connected	_____
I believe in me	We're in this together	_____
It's all going great	I make a difference	_____
I manifest my desires	Gratitude magnetizes my dreams	_____
I awake in joy	I ♥ my awesome life	_____
Laughter chases away fear	I'm part of whole	_____
I radiate joy today	Visualize whirled peas now	_____
Smiles are my response ☺	_____	_____
I uplift by shining	_____	_____
Ask, then allow it	_____	_____
Think a better thought	_____	_____
Take one step today	_____	_____

RestoringTibet.com

Mirror Mantras

Print and place on your car dashboard or opposite a mirror (such as a bathroom mirror), so you see the affirming while driving or brushing your teeth.

The Journey Home Is Sweet

Love Kindness Compassion

My Life Is Smooth and Easy-Going

RestoringTibet.com

Dalai Lama Quotes on 10 Topics

QUOTES FROM THE 14TH DALAI LAMA ON 10 TOPICS

ANGER & HATRED "Anger or hatred is like a fisherman's hook. It is very important for us to ensure that we are not caught by it."

ALL CREATURES GREAT AND SMALL "The creatures that inhabit this earth—be they human beings or animals—are here to contribute, each in its own particular way, to the beauty and prosperity of the world."

ASK THE RIGHT QUESTION "Instead of wondering WHY this is happening to you, consider why this is happening to YOU."

COMPASSION "You must not hate those who do wrong or harmful things; but with compassion, you must do what you can to stop them — for they are harming themselves, as well as those who suffer from their actions."

ENEMIES "I defeat my enemies when I make them my friends."

KNOWLEDGE "Share your knowledge. It is a way to achieve immortality."

LOOK TO EACH DAY "Let us try to recognize the precious nature of each day."

SUCCESS "Judge your success by what you had to give up in order to get it."

VIOLENCE "Through violence, you may 'solve' one problem, but you sow the seeds for another."

WORRY "If you have fear of some pain or suffering, you should examine whether there is anything you can do about it. If you can, there is no need to worry about it; if you cannot do anything, then there is also no need to worry."

RestoringTibet.com

Restoring Tibet: A News Release to Manifest

The Potala Palace
Office of the Press Secretary

FOR IMMEDIATE RELEASE:

Breaking News: The 14th Dalai Lama is in residence at the Potala Palace in Tibet.

Lhasa, Tibet — After nearly sixty years in exile in India, His Holiness the 14th Dalai Lama, Tenzin Gyatso, returned to Tibet last night, confirming widespread rumors that he was leaving Dharmasala, India, along with thousands of Tibetan refugees.

Today, the Dalai Lama issued a statement that he has returned to the Tibetan autonomous region as the spiritual leader of Tibet. "I wish to express my deepest gratitude," he added, "to the millions of people whose prayers and meditations brought me home in the spirit of kindness, compassion and reconciliation."

The founder of the "Restoring Tibet" movement, Evelyn Roberts Brooks, issued a statement from the non-profit organization's headquarters in Los Angeles, California, confirming, "The Dalai Lama has returned peacefully to his homeland after being ostracized since 1959, and on behalf of my team and all the participants in our global meditations and manifestation events, I extend a heartfelt thank you to India and her people for the many years they hosted His Holiness in exile."

Brooks explained that the two-fold purpose of the "Restoring Tibet" movement was to manifest the return to Tibet of the 14th Dalai Lama through the magnetic power of deep meditation, and to create a highly visible sign of what it looks like to transition from war, divisiveness and struggle to a higher understanding of using the laws of the mind for the greater benefit of all people.

The Dalai Lama will address the public on Saturday outside the Potala Palace. For more information, go to www.RestoringTibet.com

###

ABOUT THE AUTHOR

"Everything we say and do
is an affirmation of either fear or love."
—Evelyn Roberts Brooks

Evelyn Roberts Brooks is a writer, lightworker, and speaker. She's shared the stage with Bob Proctor ("The Secret"), Gay Hendricks, Peggy McColl, Arielle Ford, Misa Hopkins, Dr. Steve G. Jones, and other experts in personal growth and development.

She's the author of over 20 fiction and non-fiction books including "AMERICA'S NEW BREED OF FREEDOM FIGHTERS;" "YOU WERE BORN TO TRIUMPH: Create a Five-Star Life in Your Quantum Kitchen" as well as the Born to Triumph series of personal development books on individual topics; "FORGET YOUR TROUBLES: Enjoy Your Life Today;" "CALLING ALL LIGHTWORKERS;" "HEAL TOXIC FRIENDSHIPS" and other self-help books, as well as novels, including "THE DREAM SPINNERS." She's an optioned screenwriter and Nicholl Fellowship quarterfinalist.

She's also the founder of RestoringTibet.com.

Evelyn is passionate about helping others experience a transformational healing in their lives, reduce stress, heal heartache from loss, divorce, grief and trauma, and lead happier lives. With an emphasis on helping others gain clarity about the life changes they would like to make and then showing them how to expand in awareness, Evelyn inspires and encourages while making the lessons entertaining and inspiring.

Her goal is to help millions of people heal and be happier.

Be sure to stop by Evelyn's central web site evelynbrooks.com and claim free instant download access to your gift collection to relax, unwind and de-stress. It includes a 25-minute guided meditation to help you release regrets for the past and worries about the future and learn how to more easily and readily enjoy the power of living in the present moment.

Here's what Kirkus Reviews says about Evelyn's big fat juicy law of attraction book YOU WERE BORN TO TRIUMPH: Create a Five-Star Life in Your Quantum Kitchen: "Her unflagging exuberance and you-can-do-it attitude will encourage readers to remain at the buffet. This persistence pays off with nuggets of wisdom about turning one's thinking around; for example, Brooks tells of how she learned the importance of rule-breaking by drinking from a "Colored Only" fountain as a child. Wisdom like this can change lives, and Brooks' book serves up plenty. A self-improvement recipe with plenty of ingredients worth nibbling on their own."

BOOKS BY EVELYN ROBERTS BROOKS

Keep up to date by visiting booksbyevelyn.com

Nonfiction

"Liberty and Justice" Series

AMERICA'S NEW BREED OF FREEDOM FIGHTERS: With Liberty and Justice for All

WHAT WERE THEY THINKING?: Inside the Minds of Trump's Voters

WHAT TRUMP'S VOTERS WERE REALLY THINKING: The Complete Report Unedited

WHEN THEY GO LOW WE GO HIGH: How to Raise Your Vibration to Manifest What You Want

"Born to Triumph" Series

5 PROVEN METHODS TO STOP SELF-SABOTAGE

6 SECRETS FOR A NO-FAULT MARRIAGE

CALLING ALL LIGHTWORKERS: Claim Your Role in the World-Wide Awakening

CHOOSE HAPPINESS NOW

DO'S AND DON'TS FOR RECOVERING PEOPLE-PLEASERS

HEAL YOUR TOXIC FRIENDSHIPS

YOUR GRIEF RELIEF: Heal the Inner Void

YOUR HAPPINESS COMPASS

<u>Other Non-Fiction Titles</u>

BE HEALTHY, BE RICH: Secrets of Wellness and Wealth

FORGET YOUR TROUBLES: Enjoy Your Life Today

GET HAPPY TODAY: No More Excuses!

RESTORING TIBET: Global Action Plan to Send the Dalai Lama Home

YOU WERE BORN TO TRIUMPH: Create a Five-Star Life in Your Quantum Kitchen

Fiction: Adult and Young Adult

THE DREAM SPINNERS (a novel about love, loss, and second chances with a little help from the Other Side)

THE GYPSY TALISMAN

THE CALICO TAPESTRY

VAMPIRE MISCHIEF

Juvenile Fiction

PROFESSOR BUBBLES AND THE MISSING FORMULA

www.ingramcontent.com/pod-product-compliance
Lightning Source LLC
Chambersburg PA
CBHW072101280526

45788CB00006B/2359